THE TWO PRINCESSES

Photo : Marcus Adams

HER MAJESTY THE QUEEN, WITH PRINCESS ELIZABETH (*right*) AND PRINCESS
MARGARET ROSE.

THE TWO PRINCESSES

The Story of the King's Daughters

BY

FRANCES TOWERS

Copyright

NATIONAL SUNDAY SCHOOL UNION

THE PILGRIM PRESS

57–59 LUDGATE HILL, LONDON, E.C.4

PRINTED IN GREAT BRITAIN

CONTENTS

7

LIST OF ILLUSTRATIONS

I

Spring at Windsor

THE wind blustered through the night of April 21st, 1926. It blew over primrose-studded banks and swayed acres of daffodils on its hide-and-seek round of the massive grey stone towers of Windsor Castle. Overhead flew the Royal Standard, and in the Private Apartments a rather tired monarch in his sixties, King George the Fifth, and Queen Mary were sleeping.

Lights were burning in the early hours of that Wednesday morning in a house in Bruton Street at the back of Piccadilly. Although it was after three o'clock, two men were talking and smiling down at a baby—the elder the Home Secretary, Sir William Joynson-Hicks, who was there because the new Princess was in the line of succession, and the baby's excited young father, the Duke of York.

At Windsor the King and Queen were roused to hear the news that a daughter had been born to their second son, a baby who was only three removed from the Throne—her uncles Henry and George, now the Dukes of Gloucester and Kent. automatically taking a step down on the royal ladder that night.

Babies' names, especially royal ones, are seldom settled so easily as at the family debate for which the King and Queen drove to town the next day. Cablegrams, telegrams, and flowers from all over the world were arriving as they walked through an avenue of patient sightseers to meet their first granddaughter. She must be called Elizabeth after her mother —incidentally a very suitable name for an English princess —and by special request Alexandra after the King's mother, and, of course, Mary after her Daddy's mother.

Water from Palestine's River Jordan placed in Queen Victoria's silver-gilt " lily " font was poured over the baby's brow in the little private chapel in Buckingham Palace by the Archbishop of York (now Canterbury) who, eleven years later, was to crown her father and mother in Westminster Abbey while she watched for the right moment to place her coronet on her small head.

Princess Elizabeth's parents said good-bye to her when she was eight months old, leaving her with the King and Queen, and sailed for Australia and New Zealand, returning six months later in a warship, H.M.S. *Renown*, with hundreds of toys, gifts from the southern continent to their daughter. She naturally did not know the strangers who, she was told, were Daddy and Mummy, but was carried out to Buckingham Palace balcony, cheered by crowds waiting to welcome home the Duke and Duchess of York, and waved a small hand obediently.

A new life began that afternoon for the royal baby. The

first town house of the Duke and Duchess of York, 145 Piccadilly, had been made ready for them during their absence,
and the family moved in.

The King and Queen missed their granddaughter, round
whom they had made their home life for half a year. She
was taken frequently to the Palace to spend the day with them
and with her parents visited them at Windsor, Sandringham,
and Balmoral.

When two years old, Princess Elizabeth had her first worry.
She was as sorry as a child can be for the King when he fell
so ill in 1928 that his life was almost despaired of, but Char-
lotte's misery conveyed more to her. The grey parrot fretted
at not seeing its master; the day's routine, including the
morning trip on his shoulder from Palace to summer-house,
ceased suddenly, and the Princess tried to cheer it with sugar
and conversation whenever she went there.

The Princess stayed by the sea for the first time when
she visited her grandparents during the King's convalescence
at Craigweil House, Bognor. She was taken down to the beach
by her two nurses to play on the shingle and paddle, found
some sand, and Queen Mary went shopping that afternoon
in Bognor to buy her sand moulds. Her parents meanwhile
were in Norway for the marriage of Crown Prince Olaf and a
Swedish Princess, Marthe, who last spring fled with her three
children to her home country while her husband helped to
resist the German invader.

London gave the King a great welcome on his return,

11

restored to health, and the Princess was old enough on this occasion to enjoy the excitement. Thousands of people lined the streets as King and Queen drove in an open carriage through Piccadilly, and she waved frantically as they passed No. 145.

All the more puzzling that her grandfather should one day apparently fail to recognise her. It was at Balmoral and she had just arrived for a holiday at the Deeside castle. " And who is this little lady ? " the King asked her nurse, Mrs. Knight, as she trotted in. " Why, it's Lilibet," she broke in anxiously. It was her best effort at saying " Elizabeth," and became the royal family's favourite name—still sometimes used by her mother—for the child popularly known at that time as the " world's most famous baby."

Neither public ceremonies nor State entertaining kept the Duke and Duchess of York from their baby. They visited the nursery morning, noon, and night. Every stage in Princess Elizabeth's progress was watched with pride ; the Duchess compared notes with their relatives and friends. There were frequent home afternoons at No. 145 Piccadilly, when Baby was brought down to the drawing-room to play with Daddy and Mummy, who were soon on all-fours. Daddy would pick-a-back her up and down stairs. When she was out in the garden she sat on the lawn on a large rug or played with a ball, and in the nursery she was now growing out of her big play-pen. When public functions went on past their time the Duchess, with a glance at her husband to see he had taken the cue, would say

THEIR MAJESTIES WITH PRINCESS ELIZABETH (1927).

firmly, " We must get back. Princess Elizabeth will be waiting up for us." It was a happy family, with no greater pleasure than a day together at home, particularly when servants had an evening off and the Duke and Duchess waited on themselves at a cold buffet supper.

From the age of two Princess Elizabeth developed a technique with the public that astonished even her relatives. To some children crowds mean forests of legs and heads darkly blotting out the sky. To the small Princess they meant upturned faces looking towards balcony or window where someone was holding her, waving handkerchiefs, smiling, and cheering. " Aren't *you* nice ? " her answering smile seemed to say, accompanied by a friendly little wave and complete self-possession. In the garden railed off from the rest of Hyde Park at the back of the Piccadilly house, it became the natural thing to be watched on pram outings or at play. It was fun to think out occasional surprises for the onlookers who stood the other side of the railings. One day she ran up to a playmate, Lady Mairi Stewart, daughter of Lord Londonderry, brought her along like an exhibition piece, smiled at the little crowd and announced proudly, " This is Mairi."

One of the worries of the little Princess's life was making sure she had shaken hands with everybody. She never forgot the time when the King sent her back. It had been rubbed into her by her father and mother, grandfather and grandmother, an aunt and three uncles, that you must never leave anybody out ; it hurts their feelings. It was in the great Waterloo

Drawing Room at Windsor Castle, and she was told that it was her first concert. As she was only two, that did not convey much. The occasion was a Command Performance by the Royal Welsh Ladies' Choir. When it was over the King patted the golden head and told her to shake hands and say thank you. She walked up to the dais and shook a sea of hands. "Tank you" she said to each large palm extended to her, bowed over it as she took it, and at last returned. But she had missed the gentleman in the middle, who happened to be the manager, and the King sent her back.

Pets, Princess Elizabeth found, were much more interesting than toys. That was because she was not allowed to have a pet of her own until she was old enough to look after it, while she was the owner of literally tons of toys. She had begun a collection of dolls dressed in different national costumes. It is still growing, and more recent additions to it are " France " and " Marianne " in Parisian attire, presented by the children of France to herself and Princess Margaret.

Each year as the primroses unfolded in their circlet of leaves, proclaiming spring, the Princess was taken to stay at Windsor Castle with the King and Queen for Eastertide.

The real seat of the royal family from which they take their name, with the glamour of a home that is also a fort, the castle became interwoven in the child's mind with all the excitement of her birthday as it came round on April 21st. She had two identical birthday cakes apart from size, the smaller of which she cut herself while the other went to children's hospitals.

Windsor gave her first lessons in royalty, and later became linked with new privileges granted because she was a year older or because of the growing importance of her position. At Windsor, on occasion, as a baby in her pram she dismissed the old guard in the Grand Quadrangle after the new guard had been mounted, being the only royalty present. The bright red coats and flashing salute of swords excited her into jumping up and down in the pram. Afterwards she would be lifted out to walk back to the castle past saluting sentries.

On her fourth birthday Princess Elizabeth had her heart's desire of the moment—a Shetland pony given her by her father. It was the only present that could not be placed in a wonderful pile in the Oak Room at Windsor Castle. Later that day she was taken out walking and holiday-makers tried to rush the Castle gates to see her. The next morning she had her first ride on Peggy.

There was an animal present of another kind, a realistic Zoo. Each creature had been made to scale, painted in true colours, and passed by the Zoo Gardens superintendent. The elephants had movable trunks and Sam the polar bear sat up.

II

Glamis' Beacon

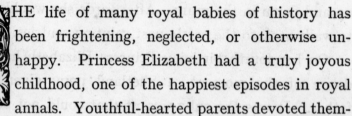HE life of many royal babies of history has been frightening, neglected, or otherwise unhappy. Princess Elizabeth had a truly joyous childhood, one of the happiest episodes in royal annals. Youthful-hearted parents devoted themselves to their small daughter; there were big boy cousins, the Princess Royal's two sons, to take her drives, play ball with her, teach her cricket and, rather unfairly in the way of small boys, make her stand for long minutes taking the salute while they were soldiers, marching, saluting, and guard changing. Wonderful castle homes were inexhaustible in their excitements, and two sets of grandparents vied with each other in giving her a good time.

There were animal friends. The King's mischievous new puppy who would bite the wire so that his study lamp would not light, Uncle David's and Uncle Henry's Scotties and Cairns, and the kennels in Windsor Great Park and elsewhere. Grandpa's racehorses and his favourite mount were beautiful to look at, but Elizabeth liked Daisy better, because she had a little red cart behind her, and looked for her each morning, once

[*Photo : Marcus Adams*

PRINCESS ELIZABETH AT THE AGE OF EIGHT

they met again, to feed her with sugar. That was at Balmoral and one had to wait till autumn to go there, but the Princess loved riding back in the cart which brought the mails to the castle. " Where are Daisy's sweeties the morn ? " the post-man would call out as he saw the small figure in the drive.

The Princess always spent part of August with her parents at her mother's old home in Scotland, Glamis Castle. Exploring the Castle was one of the thrills of life, running with other children up and down old staircases, in and out of immense rooms and through great gateways, playing in the Dutch garden, or roaming with Mrs. Knight in wooded walks. The Earl and Countess of Strathmore, her other grandparents, opened up the nurseries again, and everyone took a friendly interest in the laird's grandchild, recalling her mother at the same age.

When she was four she began to do her own shopping. Her first trip of the kind was to homely Forfar, the town near Glamis, and she asked to see books with animal pictures. The transaction was carried out without help, even to inquiring the price of the chosen book and paying from a small purse.

One day soon afterwards there was no afternoon drive outside the Castle grounds. This went on for several days, and she sometimes caught sight of little knots of people stand-ing outside the gates. Everyone was slightly mysterious, though the Princess was too small to notice it. The weather was hot, oppressive. One morning the Princess was taken in to breakfast as usual and a little later the great announcement was made to her : " You have got a baby sister." Elizabeth's face lit up. She ran excitedly into a room to see a tiny figure in a cot. " Chubby-faced," Home Secretary Clynes had called the new baby as he drove through lightning and rain to Forfar post office to make sure of the dispatch of his wire to the Lord Mayor of London, the first person outside the royal family and himself entitled to be told. That day, although the crowd was larger than before, Princess Elizabeth was allowed to drive once more through the gates, and went with Lady Strathmore to take the news to the oldest tenant and his wife, who could be relied on to tell others on the estate all about it. " I've got a new little baby sister. She is so lovely," the Princess chattered on. " I am very happy to have her."

Civic Scotland gave itself a pat on the back because the Empire's new Princess was born in Scotland of a Scottish mother, the first baby of the Blood Royal to be born north of the Tweed since James I's short-lived child, Prince Robert, 328 years ago.

That day, too, while the famous old bell of Forfar clanged out, telling the villages, the bells of Westminster Abbey were pealing and the customary royal salute of forty-one guns was fired in Hyde Park and on Tower Hill. People just shouted the Duchess's name and then cheered.

The national joy seemed like an echo of the family circle rejoicings at Glamis. The delighted young father had congratulations showered on him by neighbours, tenants, and estate employees. Lady Strathmore was proud that her granddaughter was a Glamis baby. The old Scots nurse assured callers that the child was a bonnie girl.

The little Princess considered the new arrival most opportune. In childish fashion she conveyed that it was wonderful to have a sister who would one day be old enough to order around.

She stayed up past bedtime for a thrilling sight. As dusk fell, her nurse took her to the top of the Castle. From two-mile-distant Hunter's Hill a flame leapt two hundred feet in the air, lighting the countryside. Round the beacon, she was told, people were dancing to the bagpipes in honour of the new baby who was her sister.

III

The Duke and Duchess at Home

THE new Princess at her mother's wish was given two names only, in defiance of the royal custom of calling each child after an alphabet of relatives and ancestors. The Duchess of York chose Margaret—a variation of her third name Marguerite—because of its associations with the Bowes-Lyons and links with Scottish kings from whom she is descended, and Rose after her favourite sister, Lady Rose Leveson-Gore.

Two months later the Duke and Duchess of York came back to town with their babies. Queen Victoria's children's cream silk and lace christening robe was unwrapped once more, Margaret Rose was put into it and driven to Buckingham Palace to be baptized by the Archbishop of Canterbury in the Victorian family font. Soon Margaret was crawling over the nursery floor at No. 145 Piccadilly, making so many frocks grubby that the Duchess's laundry bill would have been enormous had she not had washing and ironing equipment installed upstairs so that the children's clothes could be done at home.

This comfortable eighteenth-century, family town house was ideal once the Duchess had had gilt wire netting fixed to

PRINCESS MARGARET ROSE AT THE AGE OF FOUR.

screen the top landing, so that she did not go in fear of her babies climbing and falling over the balustrade. At present Princess Elizabeth was more interested in floors than anything else. She, and Margaret later, were allowed to do all the sweeping they liked. They soon lost interest in their own floors and discovered their mother's two beautiful drawing-rooms, which inter-communicated and were decorated alike in blue and gold so that they could be thrown into one vast room for entertaining.

Nobody minded visitors falling over babies extracting little red brushes and dustpans from behind a screen and busying themselves sweeping the carpet strenuously. Out to their own bit of Hyde Park through a gate from their garden came Princess Elizabeth daily with a long-handled broom and swept leaves in autumn, snow in winter, and gravel the rest of the year.

" Leave that to me. I'll clear that path for you," she called to the gardener, and, hatless as usual, set about her job briskly, with occasional runs to the pram to play with Margaret and the nurses.

Neither brooms, balls, nor toys could be left about for other people to pick up. The Princesses were made to tidy up after themselves, and Princess Elizabeth's favourite threat when things did not suit her, to tell the man she believed omnipotent —the King—was received with supreme indifference. After a fall one learnt to laugh, even if it hurt. Showing off in the presence of grown-ups was not worth while, as it meant banishment from the room. The reward for all this careful training was sunny-tempered children with a tremendous zest for life.

The importance of being a bridesmaid for the first time crystallised into the excitement of having a first long frock. The bride was Lady May Cambridge, daughter of Queen Mary's brother, the Earl of Athlone, now Governor-General of Canada, and the bridegroom Captain Henry Abel-Smith.

" Oh, Lilibet, you look so sweet ! " exclaimed the Duchess of York when the little Princess had taken off her pale-blue dressing-gown with its white woolly rabbits in her mother's drawing-room and was having the powder-blue velvet frock with short puff sleeves fitted by the dressmaker. With it she was to wear a plaited blue velvet Juliet cap. Everything went well until Mrs. Knight suggested that the dress could be cut down after the wedding.

" Oh no ! " exclaimed five-year-old Elizabeth in great alarm. " I would like it long always."

Driving down through London, past miles of cheering country-folk, to the Sussex village of Balcombe was an adventure to the small girl, who sat carefully with a tiny white ermine cloak over her dress. Lady May was to marry the young guardsman from her parents' country home. The Princess and another child relative, Lady Mary Cambridge, led the retinue decorously, but there was trouble at the reception when the slice of wedding-cake handed to Elizabeth proved too small for her liking.

The exploits of " my sister Margaret " began to be related

to a wide circle. Children, like grown-ups, were always in and out of No. 145, and the Princesses often went to their homes. Each Tuesday the Duchess had a drawing-room cleared, children arrived in party frocks, a dancing teacher gave lessons in standing, walking, poise, country and ballroom steps ; the Duchess invited all the youngsters to tea and they played in the nursery later. On alternate mornings Elizabeth and Margaret attended music classes at Lady Cavan's house for her daughters and neighbours' children.

Duke, Duchess, and Princesses were always singing. The parents sang with their friends after dinner, the Duchess playing the piano, and everyone full of fun. She sang often to her babies and gave Elizabeth first time-keeping lessons on the piano. Margaret could have given her no greater pleasure than she did by humming tunes before she was a year old— early evidence that she possesses a perfect ear.

At home and at Glamis the Princesses often sang hymns, nursery and folk songs, and glees with their mother. At Christmas they sang carols, and when the Duchess took them to a carol concert for the first time, Elizabeth asked specially for " The First Nowell." At Windsor they loved keeping time with the guards' band with a blind-cord tassel in the room where the royal family sat listening. In Scotland they marched up and down with the King's piper, a pair of walking bagpipes. The King installed wireless in the nursery " flat " at Sandringham so that the children could sing and dance to the music.

At church, Princess Elizabeth firmly believed in hearty

singing, and the Queen arranged where possible for sermons to be kept short, so that the whole service lasted only forty-five minutes and the little girl could stay for the address and last hymn.

Lessons became more important each year. At least three public schools were in the news at different times as the final selection for Princess Elizabeth, for whom the King and her parents had quite other ideas. So long as neither the Prince of Wales nor the Duke of York had a son, Princess Elizabeth must be regarded as ultimate heir to the Throne, and the royal custom observed of educating the heir privately.

Lessons began at the age of five. A year later the Princess had a morning routine, finishing at 11.30, when she, Princess Margaret, their nurses and sometimes their parents, went for an hour's walk together in Hyde Park, taking the quieter paths and usually unobserved. Apart from dancing there were no afternoon classes, and whatever the weather an open carriage called after lunch for the children, who drove with their nurses in one of the parks, with an umbrella held over hatless heads if it was raining.

Miss Marion Crawford took charge of the schoolroom when Elizabeth was seven and a half. This young Scotswoman had been governess to the Duchess of York's niece, Mary Leveson-Gore.

The Duchess arranged meetings with her at the parsonage when she was staying at Dunfermline, and she spent several days with the Princess to see if they took to each other. The

PRINCESS ELIZABETH OUTSIDE THE COTTAGE PRESENTED TO THE TWO
PRINCESSES BY THE PEOPLE OF WALES.

little Princess started with her that autumn in all subjects except French, for which she had a special tutor.

Margaret's capacity for mischief, practical joking, and mimicry developed an elder-sister sense in Elizabeth, who, when not under the eye of her elders or keeping an eye on her youngers, had her own outbursts.

"Oh, go and lose yourself, Margaret," Elizabeth exclaimed as she was having an interesting talk with a Court photographer, having recently been given a camera.

Margaret disappeared obediently and was nowhere to be seen when wanted, until suddenly a waste-paper basket fell and came rolling along, with a head bobbing out of it.

While their chief loves were among the menagerie of pets that began to be kept at No. 145—among them Jaggers the Cairn, Madame Butterfly the rabbit, and Dookie the Corgi—both Princesses were also attached to their dolls. Julie, given to Princess Elizabeth by her mother, was dressed in clothes to match her own, and accompanied her to important places such as Sandringham. A doll dressed as a nurse was another favourite, and there was a collection of veterans whom the Princess wheeled out in a pram each morning.

A toy table with two thimble-sized painted flower-pots on it fascinated Princess Margaret. It was a third-birthday present to her and she was sitting in a room at Glamis gazing at it and her other gifts. Suddenly she found Sir James Barrie, author of a favourite book of Elizabeth's, *Peter Pan*, looking down at her. " Is that really yours ? " he asked. She wanted to say

" yes " but politeness prompted her to reply, " It is yours and mine," and it was a great relief to find that the visitor did not claim his half.

The Princesses had their own shopping trips to buy birthday or Christmas gifts out of money saved for the purpose. They also put money by in post-office savings accounts and in home safes. One of Princess Elizabeth's chief thrills was receiving catalogues addressed to her from shops at which her clothes were bought and accounts kept in her name.

Two of the greatest events of their childhood were the gifts of real cottages, one from the Welsh people to Princess Elizabeth, the other from Aberdeen tradesmen to Princess Margaret. Princess Elizabeth had to wait over a year for " Y Bwthym Bach "—The Little House—from the time the idea was first suggested to her parents. In March 1932 it was ready and being brought by steam-wagon and trailer to London ; its thatched roof was set on fire by sparks, and it was burnt out and had to be rebuilt. This was done in time for her sixth birthday the following month, when she was given the key of the front door—but no cottage. Not until after being shown in London was the cottage brought to the Duke of York's new country home, Royal Lodge, in Windsor Great Park, and installed in the rose-garden like a Lilliputian neighbour of the big house, but it still had no furniture. It had then raised in six cities and towns over £5000, with which children's hospital beds were endowed.

That December Princess Elizabeth at last took possession

of the cottage over which she had had so many disappointments.
The architect, Mr. Morgan Willmott, and his wife were sent for ;
they met the Princess at Royal Lodge and explained everything.
How the electric fire and wireless switched on in the white-
panelled sitting-room with its blue chintz-covered chairs big
enough to sit in and table for children's tea-parties. How the
gas cooker, copper, and refrigerator worked in the blue-and-white
kitchen, how to get hot water in the pewter sink, and the secrets
of enamel-topped table cabinets. Enthralled, the little Princess was taken upstairs to see bedroom and bathroom of this
four-roomed little home, shown how the towel rail heated, bath
water turned on, and how to clean the rubber floor. The bed-
linen was pointed out to her. On it her initials had been worked.

It was an endless pleasure to the Princess to give parties
in her cottage. " Wendy's hut," which belonged to Princess
Margaret, was equally thrilling in its different way. This gabled
miniature house, with lattice windows and a porch made of
Deeside larch, big enough like the Welsh cottage for children
but not for grown-ups, was placed in the garden at Birkhall,
up at Balmoral.

IV

Two New Aunts

ADDITIONAL interest attaches to a new aunt from abroad. The Princesses helped initiate Princess Marina into British country house life. The beautiful, vivacious young woman of the Greek royal family, brought up in exile in Paris, had visited at No. 145 Piccadilly, and the two little girls knew her by sight.

One autumn morning when staying at Balmoral they learned that she was to marry Uncle George. The engaged couple arrived at Ballater Station after a tumultuous reception in London, to be greeted by the Duke and Duchess of York and a suddenly shy Elizabeth who stood on tiptoe and lifted a cheek a trifle unwillingly. Impulsive Marina did not notice this, and with a warm, unconventional hug won her friendship. The child gave an excited little skip and decided that the future aunt would be nice.

The Highland reception at Balmoral was splendid, if bewildering. There on castle lawns, colourful tartans framed by the sombre green of pines, were the Balmoral Pipers, recruited from gillies and keepers. Standing in homely fashion

36

[Photo : Marcus Adams

THE ROYAL FAMILY IN 1934.

in their porch, erect and distinguished, the smiling host and hostess were waiting, the King in a kilt, the Queen in cream lace. Princess Marina and her parents, Prince and Princess Nicholas, had no sooner entered the castle than the King led her out hand-in-hand. Little Elizabeth and Margaret laughed excitedly, pipers on the lawn ringed host and guest round, and bagpipes suddenly began to wail in the Greek Princess's ears as the wild welcome was played round and round her.

Princess Elizabeth became devoted to her during the short, crowded stay, and the invitation to be a bridesmaid at her wedding was accepted joyfully by the little girl. Princess Margaret, disappointed at being too young, was told that she should sit very near her sister in Westminster Abbey.

The royal wedding gave London an autumn of festivity and pageantry, but for the King and Cabinet those were anxious months, darkened first by the nightmare of Austria after Dolfuss's murder and, as the bells were being made to hang in West End streets, by the assassination of King Alexander of Jugoslavia, whose wife, Queen " Mignon " as she was called, was Princess Marina's cousin. Princess Elizabeth and Princess Margaret knew the little boy Peter who became King at the age of eleven, and had to be fetched home hurriedly from his English school. Europe's troubles were naturally as unreal as a remote earthquake to two small girls who came back to town from their summer holidays intensely excited at the prospect of a wedding in the family.

Silver bells decked the streets, and all over the country the

Grecian colours, sky-blue and white, hung beside the Union Jack on the morning of November 29th, 1934. Crowds were already gathering along the wedding route when Princess Elizabeth was called. She breakfasted in her dressing-gown and was soon after dressed in the frilly white-and-silver frock in which she was to act as train-bearer with Lady Mary Cambridge at Westminster Abbey.

Uniforms and wedding-guest fashions made brilliant splashes of colour against the great grey stone Abbey pillars. Up in the chancel where the royal family was sitting, five steps above the rest of the congregation, Princess Margaret was perched on a red plush footstool among the slippers and boots of her relatives, and at first was a few feet nearer the altar than the bride and her fairylike retinue of eight, all wearing white and silver. Princess Marina's brocade gown, with the rose of England traced in silver, draped gracefully as she curtsied to kings on her right and left. The solemn service began, and a few minutes later the bride's rich, musical voice uttering the words " I will " was heard in homes all over the world, for this was the first royal marriage to be broadcast.

Princess Margaret watched her elder sister walk, to her delight, almost alongside her at the point in the ceremony at which bride and bridegroom crossed the wide carpet of the chancel to kneel at the altar. The tiny figure looked like little Miss Muffet as she sat quietly trying to attract her sister's attention and to avoid that of the adults above it. Princess Elizabeth ignored her until Margaret started twiddling her thumbs, when she shook her head solemnly. All movement from the footstool ceased.

A wedding reception at Buckingham Palace was a new experience for both little Princesses. They watched the Duke of Kent lead their new aunt to her place in one of the handsome State reception rooms, magnificent with gold plate filled with white flowers decorating a score of round tables. The children, like every grown-up guest, each received a wedding flower favour. They saw the Duchess of Kent cut the first slice of the cake with her husband's sword. Later, hand in hand they scampered across the inner quadrangle, throwing silver tokens and rose petals after the honeymoon State coach as it drove the couple off to Paddington Station with an escort of Life Guards.

Less than a month later Aunt Marina passed with honours as an addition to the King's Christmas house party for the family at Sandringham.

Princess Elizabeth enjoyed Christmas even more than usual, thanks to her new party frock. Aunt Marina had married just in time, for though still fond of her first bridesmaid's frock, now three years old, she was getting tired of it for best. The Duchess of York had the Princesses' frocks made with such deep hems and wide turnings that they sometimes felt they would never grow out of them. The powder-blue velvet bridesmaid's dress of 1931 had been let down and down for successive Sandringhams. The novelty of an ankle-length frock having worn off, the little Princess was very pleased because the new one was knee-length, and very proud of its silver foundation under the stiffened white tulle. Her fellow train-bearer, Lady Mary Cambridge, wore hers, too, at Sandringham on Christmas Day.

The Duchess of York considered that for ordinary occasions children's clothes should be simple and serviceable and strongly disapproved of costly or elaborate styles. Sometimes Queen Mary gave her own little-worn, beautiful pastel-coloured velvet and silk gowns to the young mothers in the royal family to be cut down for frocks for their children.

Relatives, too, made clothes for the royal children. Queen Mary sometimes knitted them jumpers. As they grew older their mother took them to a Sloane Street children's dressmaker for most of their clothes.

Silver Jubilee Year dawned while the Princesses were still at Sandringham. The King, his children, grandchildren, and the wider family of Empire drew near to each other in those serenely happy domestic celebrations of the months that followed. The love and appreciation shown him made him sure as never before of the friendship of the people he ruled. He talked and moved among them with a grateful confidence.

Princess Elizabeth, nine that April, took a small official part in Empire celebrations. Her portrait appeared on various Silver Jubilee stamps; it was also used on Canada's bank bills. Fair-skinned, blue-eyed, with regular features, happy-natured but serious and quaintly dignified, the Princess in appearance and character was very like Queen Mary, while temperamentally, impish little Princess Margaret was developing into a junior

SILVER JUBILEE OF KING GEORGE V. AND QUEEN MARY.

The King and Queen (then the Duke and Duchess of York) with the two Princesses and the
Duke and Duchess of Kent leaving St. Paul's Cathedral after the Thanksgiving Service.

edition of the Duchess of York, a merry, unselfish, and most lovable child.

Even the Princesses, young as they were, realised that Grandpa tired easily. It was only by taking elaborate precautions to save him from fatigue that he succeeded in never disappointing the public and carrying out the full Silver Jubilee programme.

For the first time the Princesses went inside St. Paul's Cathedral, for whose dome they had watched when driving to the station to entrain for Sandringham. It was May 6th, 1935, and the cathedral was massed with the Nation's and Empire representatives giving thanks to God for a ruler who " has come to be not the King only but the father of his people."

They sat right under the dome and were so fascinated that before that day was over they had made their parents promise to take them in the whispering gallery, which they did in the following year. Once again at this service a footstool was provided for Princess Margaret, but Princess Elizabeth had a chair like the grown-ups.

Although it was the first time that the young Princesses had attended a cathedral service, they had been taken regularly to church each Sunday morning from the time that they were old enough to understand simple prayers and hymns. Their religious training received much thought and personal attention from their parents. The Duchess of York told her children Bible stories much as Lady Strathmore, her mother, had told them to her when she was small. By the age of six she knew them well and in detail. It was the Duchess, too, who taught her little daughters to say their first prayers.

That autumn the Princesses realised that there was to be another new aunt and that at last Margaret, now five, was old enough to be a bridesmaid. It was the turn of their soldier uncle, Henry. They had seen his fiancée, Lady Alice Scott, in Scotland; she was fond of country life and did not care for towns. She was most knowledgeable about horses and dogs, and the Princesses felt that her qualifications as a relative were of the highest.

Princess Elizabeth's luck was in. For two years running she would have a new Christmas party frock. The wedding-day was to be November 6th, Westminster Abbey was the inevitable choice for the ceremony, and Lady Alice decided that she and her bridesmaids should all be dressed in pearl colour. A young Englishman who had built up a name as a fashionable dressmaker and was recommended to Lady Alice, inexperienced in London ways, by her sister-in-law, made the bride's gown of pearl-tinted satin and the matching brides-maids' frocks of pearl-tinted tulle over satin. Each Princess had a little bracelet of Alexandra roses to match her wreath and neckline trimming.

Fittings were not the only excitement that autumn. The Princesses learned that they had a new cousin, Prince Edward, and that while he was to be named after the Prince of Wales, he was a " proper George " according to everyone at No. 3 Belgrave Square, the image of his father from the very first.

46

The arrangements at Westminster Abbey for Uncle Henry's wedding were complete when they suddenly had to be cancelled owing to the death of Lady Alice's father, the Duke of Buccleuch. It was decided that the ceremony should take place privately on the chosen day in the chapel at Buckingham Palace.

The Duchess of York wondered if Margaret would keep her shoes on. There were three awkward steps up to the chapel and Margaret was to hold one side of the bride's four-yard train, wearing court-shoe slippers of gold without elastic, because it showed.

Princess Margaret demonstrated what she could do, and without mishap walked beside little Anne Hawkins, the bride's niece, leading the six other bridesmaids from the drawing-room in which the procession assembled.

A fortnight later another family gathering took place at the Palace for the christening of the Duke and Duchess of Kent's baby, Edward George Nicholas Paul Patrick. The historic family robe again had a brief outing.

That Christmas for the last time George the Fifth played the rôle of squire of Sandringham and host to his family. Although he had planned a more wonderful time for the children than ever, as if aware that next year he would not be there, things were different. The two new daughters-in-law, the Duchess of Gloucester and the Duchess of Kent, were guests, but the Duke and Duchess of York, without whom it was difficult to imagine Christmas, were absent. The little Princesses spent the festival knowing that their mother was very ill at Royal Lodge

47

with influenzal pneumonia and that their father was with her. Their nurseries at Sandringham were decorated; they put round their Christmas cards and also crackers which they pulled with callers, and helped distribute gifts to employees and tenants. In the ballroom there was a thirty-foot Christmas-tree, and the new aunts worked their hardest to prevent them missing their parents, always diplomatically ready for a game of hide-and-seek, and when it was too dark to be outdoors, reading to them in the great hall by the big log fire, laden with birch logs which the Queen liked because they do not spark. The Princesses saw as much as usual of Grandpa, who loved them to talk to him when he was not too tired. He rode and walked, went to church on Christmas morning, joining in the singing with the choir of village boys and girls, gave dinner-parties and had relays of guests, so that someone was always coming or going.

Yet though he was as good company and interested in everything as ever, the grown-ups in the family house party were prepared for the loss that the New Year was to bring, for as one of his great friends said, " I had a feeling through the autumn that he was ready for the long journey that he was so soon to take."

[*Photo : Studio Lisa*

PRINCESS ELIZABETH AT THE AGE OF TEN.

A photograph taken in the garden at 145 Piccadilly with the Corgi, Jane. The Princess wears
a pale mauve silk frock with a white frilly collar.

V

Last Salute

THE Duchess of York, now convalescent, sat with her two little daughters. It was January 19th. Yesterday the children had been at Sandringham. Everyone had looked solemn. Mrs. Knight had packed their clothes and brought them home. Grandpa, who had been staying indoors with a slight bronchial cold, had suddenly become very ill, and the doctors put it down to his heart.

Now, like the rest of the Empire, the children and their mother sat in arm-chairs listening-in to the latest reports of the King's fight for life. Sometimes a telephone call came from that anxious group of waiting relatives at Sandringham.

In London, too, people waited in bitter cold, each day and night, to read the bulletins posted outside the palace. It was hard to realise that a few days ago the invalid had been well and full of jokes.

It was on a happy note that that royal life ended, on January 20th, just five minutes before midnight, sending people sorrowfully to bed. His Jubilee provided him with consoling last memories. In his Christmas broadcast he had talked of the

" spontaneous offering of loyalty—and may I say love "
showered on him and his " dear wife " in that unforgettable
year. All the Christmas holiday he had been touched by the
" warm and generous remembrance of the man himself," the
wonderful greetings to him from all over the Empire on Christmas morning, the sympathy with him over the sister Victoria,
whose death just before Christmas had grieved him greatly.

While he was dying, Italy was bombing Abyssinia, and in
Berlin, Hitler fervently described the ardent New Year German
desire for goodwill and co-operation. The worn old squire of
Sandringham was grateful that he left his peoples at peace.

Like everybody else the little Princesses felt sorry for
Queen Mary. The Prince of Wales, who was now King Edward,
and whom they admired enormously, was at Sandringham,
and her other sons and daughter also. National sorrow found
dramatic expression. The Princesses were told that in London
Big Tom, the bell of St. Paul's, was tolling all day and that
guns had been fired for each of the seventy years of their
grandfather's life. The other end of Windsor Great Park, the
Castle's Royal Standard flew at half mast, a thing that only
happened when the King of England died.

The coffin, draped with the Royal Standard, was taken to
the village church, where Queen Mary went alone at midnight
to pray beside it. It was brought to London for four days'
lying-in-state in ancient Westminster Hall, where only last
May the Lords and Commons had congratulated King George
on his Silver Jubilee. Four officers guarded the coffin and four

Gentlemen-at-Arms stood side by side before it, and the fifteen thousand people who filed past each hour were at one time walking by the late King's four sons, who changed places with the Gentlemen-at-Arms to watch over their father's body.

Princess Elizabeth was taken there by her mother and Queen Mary to pay tribute to the grandfather who had been so big a figure in her young life. Beside her stood kings and crown princes come to London for the funeral, while the unending queue continued on its snake-like way.

George the Fifth was laid in the burial-place of the kings at Windsor nine days after his death. Princess Elizabeth was present but it was decided to spare her the ordeal of riding in the slow procession behind the coffin through London streets, and to let her join the mourners at Paddington Station.

The two little sisters saw the coffin, surmounted by crown, sceptre, and orb, pass by No. 145 Piccadilly on a gun carriage. Princess Margaret in a little grey frock came out alone with her nurse on to the purple-draped balcony to curtsy, a small forlorn figure, while her elder sister remained behind a window dressed ready for departure from the tradesmen's entrance, where she could avoid the crowds.

On the station platform she saw her cousins, Viscount Lascelles and his brother Gerald, at the salute. She joined her mother and Queen Mary. The new King waited for the coffin to be carried into the train, helped his mother tenderly into the saloon, stooped down to Elizabeth looking tall and slim in black tam and black coat, and handed her in. Others followed. The senior guard waved his green flag as if it were an ordinary journey. Hymn tunes played by the band died away. The train moved forward in a sorrowing rhythm, the lament of the pipers playing "Flowers of the Forest" following the body in a last salute.

St. George's Chapel, Windsor, was so filled with flowers and sad pageantry that few people saw the little wreath of snowdrops and pink tulips worded "from his grandchildren, Lilibet, Margaret, Edward, George, and Gerald."

Much as the Empire mourned a ruler who had carried through a job for which he was never trained with a sense of duty that "amounted to genius," George the Fifth's real memorial was in the hearts of his own family, for even remote relatives had numerous tales of kindnesses and help that were the true measure of the man who was also a king.

A seaside holiday at Eastbourne helped the Duchess of York to convalesce and to blow away sad thoughts. The Princesses took spades, pails, and Dookie, the Welsh Corgi, bred from an old sheepdog strain. The little Princess walked her dog on the downs each day, brushed and fed him, well aware that if she did not carry out her part of the contract to look after her pets properly herself, she would not be allowed to have them.

It was a strange year with Windsor Castle deserted and no Easter holiday there. Queen Mary spent the festival as a guest at Royal Lodge. The new King entertained at Fort Belvedere. Buckingham Palace had no king; Queen Mary had not yet moved out. Spring provided Princess Elizabeth

[Photo : Studio Lisa

UNDER THE SILVER BIRCHES IN THE GARDENS OF ROYAL LODGE.
The sisters are knitting for the troops.

with one great thrill, a tour of the mammoth new liner *Queen Mary*. She inspected the children's playroom, slid down the chute, set a Mickey Mouse film in motion, and asked for a souvenir sailor doll for Margaret, then returned to the deck in time to see Uncle David salute the great ship from the air by circling and dipping his plane.

That summer Margaret and she discovered picnicking. They drove to Buckingham Palace to picnic in the gardens by the reed-edged lake, put sandwiches in a little case on her bicycle at Windsor, and when they went to Scotland picnicked with their parents on the sands near Glamis. That year two Corgis accompanied them, Dookie and Jane; the little bitch was so obedient that she came to be preferred for town life and Dookie to be left at Windsor with the Labradors and Tibetan lion dog.

The simple, uneventful times spent by the royal children at their parents' country homes were gloriously happy. They loved riding as well as their walks and outdoor parties. Far from being the sort of children who want their elders to keep them amused, the little Princesses were always interested and full of youthful activities. Having been brought up simply, they enjoyed everything.

Guests of the Duke and Duchess, painting the picture of their home life, paid tribute to the fact that it was "so ordinary" —so like the life of any other family. Herein lay the charm of a visit to this royal couple.

Plans were in progress for the coronation of King Edward

next May. The constitutional crisis that developed was shortly to reach its height and its effects were to be far reaching.

The King stayed on at Fort Belvedere. It was there that, on December 10th, he abdicated, after having reigned only 325 days.

The Princesses learned that evening that their father and mother had become King and Queen. Too excited to sleep they jumped out of bed and two little heads appeared at the window under the blind. There was an electric feeling, indoors and out. They watched crowds and callers. Daddy had gone that day to Fort Belvedere; Mr. Baldwin to Marlborough House. Sir John Simon went to Fort Belvedere and the Duke of Kent to Marlborough House. Looking tired and depressed, their father returned home at midnight, King and Emperor. Long before that the little sisters had fallen asleep.

When they woke up the following day, their heads full of the changes about to happen to them, they learned that Uncle David was going away. Lessons were a supreme effort. They wanted to watch all the interesting arrivals. There was a stream of Court officials, statesmen, and messenger boys.

Mr. Baldwin and his pipe arrived. He knocked the pipe out on the base of the pillar while people cheered. The children saw Lord Cromer call, they knew that as Lord Chamberlain he was head of the King's (their father's) household. Guardsmen came. Then Uncle Henry appeared. He, too, got cheers. He stayed till after tea, and he and Daddy drove away together, Mummy told them that they had gone to a good-bye dinner-party being given by Daddy for Uncle David at Royal Lodge at which Queen Mary, her four sons, and daughter were to spend a last evening together. King Edward left the party for about an hour to make his farewell broadcast to the nation from Windsor Castle.

The Princesses knew that the next day their father was to be proclaimed King by the heralds and that by then their uncle would have left England.

That was another wakeful night. Princess Elizabeth, astute and inquiring, was most concerned with the change of homes that awaited them. Buckingham Palace, Windsor Castle, Balmoral, and Sandringham were theirs. But she could not bear the idea of giving up Royal Lodge, which was so nice for riding because the ponies could be brought to the front door, and where they had so many of their pets. One of her first requests to the father who was now King was that they should still go there for week-ends, a promise that was given and kept, in spite of the surprise it caused in Court circles.

By the time the Princesses were called the next morning, King Edward had sailed in a destroyer for the Continent.

VI

Moving in to the Palace

CHRISTMAS brought a return to normality, which the new King and Queen welcomed all the more for their children because life was soon to be as fantastic as a fairy tale. The Coronation was already looming; preparations were to go on as before, only a different King would be crowned and a Queen as well.

Sandringham seemed lost without George the Fifth, and driving from Wolferton Station brought sad memories of his last days there. It was a quiet Christmas. Queen Mary joined them. The Duke and Duchess of Kent stayed in London. The family, the Princesses felt, had shrunk suddenly.

Their mother was careful to do everything as grandma did it and not seem to be taking over, as she had a horror of hurting people's feelings. Ever since she or the Princesses could remember, Queen Mary had been mistress of Sandringham. She consulted her about each thing and the Princesses followed suit. She would go arm-in-arm with her through the doors to avoid going first because she was queen.

There was a London phone call for the King on his return

ROYAL GARDENERS.

On the terrace at Royal Lodge, Windsor, with Carol in the barrow, just off for a morning's
gardening.   They are wearing little rust-coloured jackets and practical plaid skirts.

with his family to the great creeper-hung house from church on Christmas morning. Just before dinner was announced— served midday so that the Princesses could have their turkey, chestnut stuffing, flaming plum-pudding, and brandy sauce with the grown-ups—their father reappeared with the news that Prince Edward had a sister, born that Christmas morning, and that the Duke and Duchess of Kent were going to call her after Sandringham's first royal hostess, Queen Alexandra.

The Coronation and the move to Buckingham Palace were the most debated family topics that holiday. The Princesses visualised the coming centuries-old ceremony as a glorified royal wedding, much more " wonderful and lovely." They would not only have new frocks but coronets designed with heraldic crosses and fleurs-de-lis to show that they were king's daughters, and purple velvet trains called " robes " hung from the shoulders with gold cords and trimmed with ermine and gold. They had carried brides' trains ; now they were to be taught to manage their own.

Their mother was to have a crown made for her out of diamonds in the royal collection, including the greatest historical stone in existence, Koh-i-Noor, as there was nothing suitable for her among existing crowns. The gems were to be set in platinum. Their father's crowns would come out of the glass case at the Tower. He would be crowned with the gold Crown of England, made for Charles II and called St. Edward's, and would never wear it again. For use he would have the Imperial State Crown, which showed him to be an emperor and contained the Black Prince's ruby and the Cullinan diamond. By the stroke of the pen with which King Edward signed away the Throne, the Princesses had become two very important people, despite their youth. Elizabeth, nearly eleven, was well aware that but for her sex she would have been Prince of Wales, and that as heir presumptive she had certain privileges. She also realised that it was more important than ever for her to work hard with Miss Crawford and the tutors coaching her in special studies, languages, and history.

As in all matters affecting their children's upbringing, the King and Queen constantly discussed the Princesses' progress in the schoolroom. Where practicable, they liked other children to share the Princesses' classes. The royal children had had the team spirit developed in them from very early years and worked well with others, always quick to praise when another child's achievement outshone their own.

Both Princesses love reading and Princess Elizabeth possesses a fine large bookcase to which Queen Mary has been a constant contributor. The Princess groups her collection intelligently under different subjects. She has a great many fairy tales, children's classics, and books about horses, a good collection of poetry with a well-used Shakespeare, most of whose plays she now knows, and several of Sir Walter Scott's books, of which she is fond because the author stayed at Glamis and described scenes she knows well.

The gulf between eleven years and not quite seven years is immense. The Princesses' days were entirely different, and during term they now saw little of each other except at breakfast and bedtime. Princess Elizabeth spent the greater part of the day with Miss Crawford, Princess Margaret was still in the nursery with Mrs. Knight. Each child had many friends of her own age, but on holidays and at week-ends they were inseparable—Princess Elizabeth very much the elder sister, in command, kindly ; Princess Margaret mischievous, an incessant little talker, as she is to this day, argumentative, but obedient.

Plans for moving into the Palace without delay were carried out in the New Year. The Princesses forgot their sorrow at the approaching departure from No. 145 Piccadilly when the King promised that when they had learnt to swim he would have swimming pools built both at the Palace and Royal Lodge. They started lessons immediately under the Bath Club children's instructor, Miss Daly, and in two years had made such progress that each won awards for style and speed in the club's annual contests.

The immediate Palace problem was that of suitable rooms for the children. It was a long time since a young family had lived there, but the King and Queen neither wanted to spend a lot of money, nor to have the Palace turned upside down for decorations when Coronation entertaining was about to begin. They decided that nothing need be done to the rooms they were to use, but that a suite must be prepared properly for their daughters.

It consisted of five second-floor rooms near Queen Mary's old suite, now to be occupied by their mother, on the Piccadilly

side of the Palace. The rooms opened on to the corridor in
such a way as to form a self-contained flat. There were a day-
and a night-nursery. And there was Princess Elizabeth's
study-sitting-room, fitted with power points so that she could
have an electric fire, and with a special reading lamp and
telephone receiver for her desk. The walls were painted pale
cream, and the Princess was to have her tea there each day
with Miss Crawford and do her homework in it, undisturbed
by Princess Margaret who would be playing in the nursery.

The Palace corridors, immensely long, with old-fashioned
cerise or red carpet that was soft to fall on, became the Princesses' favourite playground. The King, though now a very
busy man with less time for his family, sometimes gave Margaret
a ride on his back up and down the great carpeted stretches.
Each afternoon Palace officials, unaccustomed to children, were
startled to hear running and shrieks of laughter as the sisters
raced each other tirelessly up and down three glorious floors.
Later that year, when the first Buckingham Palace Girl Guide
Company was formed, the Princesses found the corridors ideal
for signalling practice. Queen Victoria's home, in which she
had brought up her nine, was once again a children's palace.

Soon the Princesses discovered that to live at THE Palace
was far more than getting used to a new home or staying at a
castle. Kingship functioned there. It was a nerve centre of
Empire and of Europe. Every day their parents, separately
or together, gave audiences to Cabinet Ministers, ambassadors,
foreign statesmen. By signing papers the King set laws in

THE TWO PRINCESSES WITH THE PENGUINS AT THE LONDON ZOO.

motion. Sometimes the Great Seal was used. The Palace's own post office needed to be the most modern in the country to deal with the King's and Queen's enormous mails and the never ceasing cables and telegrams. Their father required more offices and secretaries than at Piccadilly. The Palace had very up-to-date telephone equipment. The King could ring up his family and Cabinet by means of private lines not operating through an exchange, so that his conversations could not be overheard.

The Queen had her own Private Secretary to deal with her increased correspondence, but her Ladies-in-Waiting continued to deal with the more personal of Her Majesty's letters, as also with the Princesses' correspondence.

Princess Elizabeth was beginning to receive letters from children all over the world. Her " fan " mail was so large that it took a lot of time to deal with it. Many of the letters were appeals from suffering children such as the Chinese refugees fleeing from the Japanese battle area, orphaned, starving, cold, and in rags. Care was always taken on the Princess's behalf to see that something helpful was done.

Every day the Queen refused requests that the Princess should attend public functions, such as the opening of a children's hospital ward. Most of the invitations to private parties were also refused. The King decided that until she was sixteen she must live as much like an ordinary child as possible.

The Queen insisted on simple dishes for the royal nursery and schoolroom meals, at which the Princesses were waited on

by their own two scarlet-liveried footmen. At ten o'clock each
morning the chef sent upstairs to Mrs. Knight one of three
morocco-bound books, containing the day's suggested menus
for the nursery. The Princesses had the kind of food served
in every English home, nothing rich or extravagant—boiled
mutton and caper sauce, steak and kidney pudding, boiled beef
and dumplings, stewed rabbit, calves' liver and bacon. They
liked Irish stew, one of the few dishes their father disliked.
They were very fond of steam puddings, and for an occasional
treat were given a meringue or ice, at other times the only
sweet that appeared was compote of figs and farola pudding.
In summer they often had jellies.

The only difference between their meals and those of scores
of other homes was that a menu written in French was placed
on the table. In this way they learnt naturally the international
language of the cuisine.

VII

Coronation Year

IN March 1937 the five-months' non-stop Coronation programme began, the crowning coming as the central event on May 12th. King and Queen realised that the Princesses must play their part in the national celebrations, little as they liked this whirl of pageantry, popular adulation, and unreal atmosphere for their daughters.

The strong sense of duty to the public possessed by both the King and Queen, found full and a new expression in Coronation Year. The Princesses could not fail to be influenced by the spirit of untiring service shown throughout by their parents, and the seeds of fine qualities, sown long ago, came into visible being in those stirring days.

With a fine example always before them and a home life that was, for all its allowance for spontaneity, a training in unselfishness and obedience, the Princesses had unconsciously and naturally acquired thoughtfulness for others, sympathy, and unfailing courtesy. Those who saw them at some of the many functions of Coronation Year were greatly attracted by their quaint childish dignity, engaging politeness, and friendly manner.

71

One March afternoon the King and Queen gave their first Palace party. Princess Elizabeth and Princess Margaret were the only children there. They had never attended such an important party before and they stood in their matching dusk-pink frocks beside their parents at the top of the imposing Grand Staircase.

The Queen was so busy that the Princesses rarely saw her alone. Sometimes she almost dropped with tiredness during the fittings of her Coronation clothes at the Palace, and the King, who looked in frequently from his study, would bring her a cup of tea while the fitter pinned and the designer adjusted stiff and stately folds of fabric.

Life in those hectic pre-Coronation days had its lighter side. " Oh, mummy," said Princess Elizabeth one day, " you must come and look at this enormous box."

" Darling, I'm just getting into my dress. Can't you wait a minute ? "

" No, mummy. I can't wait one minute."

So, in response to her daughter's firm reply, the Queen hastily gathered up armfuls of the most important dress of a decade, the costly gold-embroidered ivory satin Coronation gown which, after she had worn it for her crowning as Queen-Empress, would pass into Empire history and become a museum relic. She ran after her dancing-eyed daughter into her bedroom where a large box containing the King's Coronation robe stood in a corner out of the way.

From the box two jackanape figures jumped, Princess

THEIR MAJESTIES KING GEORGE VI. AND QUEEN ELIZABETH, WITH PRINCESSES
ELIZABETH AND MARGARET ROSE, IN THEIR CORONATION ROBES.

Margaret and a little brown Corgi, disentangling themselves from the coverings that protected the yards of purple velvet for which English silkworms had been busily spinning for months.

The dressmakers pursued the Queen down to Windsor Castle during her Easter holiday. With the Coronation less than a month off there was no respite. The endless fittings went on ; so did the endless entertaining. Tired as the Queen was, she had to give house-parties each week-end so that Cabinet ministers, diplomats, and officers of State could come and talk over arrangements for the great day with the King.

The Princesses enjoyed the family seat being re-opened. It had been closed for nearly two years. King Edward, now the Duke of Windsor, had always gone to Fort Belvedere and never used the Castle. Princess Elizabeth was allowed to plan her birthday programme for herself—she was eleven that April 21st—and to seat her guests where she chose at her party in the Oak Room at which she took the head of the table.

When the royal family returned to town after Easter it was to see splendid decorations already in place or going up on lamp-posts, kerbs, refuges or flung from windows across streets, and huge crowds occupying the thoroughfares day and night, reducing traffic to a crawl, out to see all the sights and to cheer any royal car wildly.

Abbey rehearsals went on apace. The King and Queen were instructed in the meaning of the rites—the Queen had not attended the last Coronation and had no first-hand knowledge like the King of the elaborate and highly symbolical ceremonies of the recognition, anointing, investing, crowning, and homage.

Their little daughters, who must walk with dignity, in their robes, up the length of Westminster Abbey to seats in the Royal Box, were rehearsed by Queen Mary and the Princess Royal. They were taken to the Abbey and made to walk either side of their aunt, with Queen Mary as critic behind them, until they knew what to do.

The Queen knew perfectly well that while the Princesses might manage their velvet robes which hung like trains behind them, they would be certain to trip over dresses that touched the ground. She refused to follow the custom of trailing Coronation frocks for royal children and had her daughters' dresses of white lace made ankle-length.

Their small ermine-bordered purple robes with triple bars of gold arrived at the Palace a fortnight before the day. Princess Margaret's rested about eighteen inches on the ground, Princess Elizabeth's was a little longer in proportion to her height.

London never slept through the night that turned into May 12th. Palace lights burned long before dawn. Crowds began to fill the pavements where some determined souls had spent the night on camp stools, troops took up places along the royal route. Faces appeared at every office window; tiers of specially constructed seats, for which high prices had been paid, filled nearer the time. The great wooden barriers, enclosing the Coronation area like a walled city, were shut.

Driving through beflagged streets that rang to the echo

with cheers, the Princesses arrived in a Cinderella-like glass coach at the Abbey, whipped their robes on to their left arms as they had been shown, picking up their frocks with the same movement and showing bare legs above socks, and reached the Royal Gallery safely. Princess Elizabeth adjusted Princess Margaret's little train and nearly pulled it off. The smaller child stood most of the time on tiptoe, asking innumerable questions throughout the three hours' rites.

The Princesses looked down intently at their father, isolated from them, from the vast congregation, and even from the Queen, lonely central figure in all that blaze of colour. As they watched and listened, millions of unseen listeners were there in spirit, sitting by radio sets in their drawing-rooms, hearing the Primate present the King for recognition to the people, and the King repeating with the familiar, characteristic slight pause between every two or three words, " All this—I promise to do." They watched him uncovered make his solemn oath, saw the anointing, investing and then the splendid moment of crowning—moving ceremonies, the deep meaning of which was conveyed for the first time by wireless to every home.

The Queen's crowning afterwards found the Princesses at the alert. The Archbishop of Canterbury placed the new crown on her head. It seemed as if the famous Koh-i-Noor, which, traditionally, women alone can wear without courting ill-luck, had trapped a thousand fierce darts of intense light. At the same moment each child put on her little fairy-tale coronet, and with a rustling sound in perfect unison the peeresses simultaneously turned their coronets the right way up and placed them on their brows.

It was the kind of transporting event that leaves one in a semi-ecstatic state from which descent to everyday level is difficult. The carriage processions drove back through seas of cheers to the Palace, and the crowds stayed on outside the gates all day, with more thunderous cheers when the King and Queen came on to the balcony with their crowns, and the Princesses nodded heads and coronets gaily.

The two months that followed were just like a continuation of the Coronation itself, with State drives, mammoth youth displays, and an official tour of Scotland for which King and Queen and their daughters stayed at Mary Queen of Scots' Palace, Holyroodhouse. The elder Princess accompanied her parents to the naval review.

The King and Queen discussed the best method of settling their daughters down again. Each week-end during Coronation summer they went to Royal Lodge, where, without a Court of royal household officials and attendants a King and Queen and their children become just an ordinary family party leading a simple country life.

[Photo : Studio Lisa

A FAMILY GROUP AT ROYAL LODGE.

VIII

Pets at Royal Lodge

ROYAL LODGE was planned by its owners for open-air activities and simple living. Its position, deep in Windsor Great Park, remote from motor roads, made it an ideal near-London sovereign's week-end retreat. State papers could be brought from town by dispatch riders with little delay. Important visitors could pay formal calls at Windsor Castle, as the King could reach the Castle in a very few minutes to receive them.

The charming three-storied Georgian house, which the Queen had had painted a blush pink outside, is screened from week-end sightseers by lilacs, firs, and plane trees, a large circular garden, mostly wild, and rustic wood fence. Its generous supply of large, low windows give it a pleasant look of basking in sunshine. Framed by the rose-garden on the left, the thatched roof of Princess Elizabeth's Welsh cottage is visible, with flower beds all round in which the Princesses planted for themselves rose trees, primulas, polyanthus, and bulbs.

Since their parents occupied Royal Lodge, the Princesses have been allowed to have more dogs. Their father used the kennels to breed Labradors. In addition they had Shetland collies, the now familiar Welsh sheep-dogs—Corgis—which they had helped to save from oblivion, and the Tibetan lion dog. These were the family's four most favoured breeds. To reach the kennels the Princesses, hatless, in little washable print frocks, and unattended even by their nurse, raced about half a mile outside Royal Lodge gates through a stretch of park and paddock to a little colony of cottages where the King's employees lived.

The dogs bounded out to greet them. There were Spark and Flash, the pretty Shetland collies; Scrummy, Mimsey, and Stiffy, the Golden Labradors.

Woodsmen and stable and kennel hands talked to the Princesses as to any other small girls. They would shout out to Margaret, " Keep away from the fire. You'll get smoked out," when she amused herself with a bonfire, and they never thought of saying " Princess." It did not occur to them that the King had a crown. He paid them wages and if driven to comment they observed in their slow, deliberate country fashion that he was a " beautiful gentleman." And they knew perfectly well that if anyone was sick or in trouble, royal servants would be round with food and other practical help from the Queen.

The Princesses would chase back across those silent green acres, peopled by the King's men, who saw they came to no harm. Even at week-ends, there was seldom a stranger there in the mornings. Whenever Princess Margaret saw a big tree stump she climbed on to it, and grown-ups might have had a shock to hear the King's younger daughter shouting out: " I'm the king of the castle. Get out you dirty rascal." Hardly a rhyme that one would associate with royalty, though it often brought a smile to the gnarled faces of the men sweeping paths or sawing branches.

Every morning during holidays, two ponies " called " at the front door of Royal Lodge, brought by the groom for the Princesses' hour and a half's ride in the park. Sometimes the King's mount was also brought round. The Queen never rode. Although she had done so a great deal in the past, she had lost the taste for it and had not mounted a horse for years. Riders meeting the two little girls on horseback would salute them.

" We haven't seen that lady since we were here in April last year," Princess Elizabeth once commented. She was right, as usual. Riding helped to train her naturally good memory and powers of observation.

Neither Princess rode on Sunday. The little girls were brought up to regard it as a rest day for everybody.

" Horses must have a holiday," Princess Elizabeth would say with conviction.

She might have added grooms, too ; and her riding-master, Owen, was grateful to the King for insisting that Sunday must be a day of rest for man and beast. Princess Margaret was anxious that the ponies should enjoy their holiday. She had read about pit ponies and told people that " they could not have much fun, living underground." Princess Elizabeth's favourite book at this period was the classic tale of a horse, *Black Beauty*.

So on Sunday morning the tables were turned and the Princesses called on their ponies. They had three now—Peggy, Princess Elizabeth's first, on which she had given Margaret first lessons; Snowball; and the elder Princess's new pony, Comet.

The stables were near the kennels and the Princesses walked there after church with pieces of carrot and lumps of sugar in their pockets.

Sometimes the royal family walked all the way to Windsor Castle to attend the service at St. George's Chapel. It was a good tramp up the rightly named Long Walk. At other times they went to the Chapel Royal in the grounds of Royal Lodge.

Sunday dinner was taken on the terrace when possible. On Sunday afternoon the King liked to drive his wife and children himself in an open car; Windsor Forest was a favourite haunt, and they would get out and walk there. On their return there was often a tea-party on the lawn at Royal Lodge, with probably Prince Edward and Princess Alexandra as guests.

The Princesses were both strong and full of energy and had escaped all the usual childish complaints. They seldom caught colds and the explanation lay in the programme of exercise laid out for them.

The swimming pool at Royal Lodge, though a great source of pleasure, was not built purely for amusement. The King

[*Photo : Studio Lisa*

PRINCESS ELIZABETH AT HER LESSONS.
She wears a cotton print frock, multi-coloured, with coral and crystal beads.

took a firm view that every child should be taught swimming in self protection, and he expected his children to work at their strokes so that they became really strong swimmers. The pool had a little flat-roofed pavilion for undressing, and cement sides, all painted the same pink as the house, making an effective contrast with the blue floor under the water. A diving-board was provided, and on hot days the Princesses and their friends were in and out most of the afternoon.

Both royal children became keen cyclists at an early age, taking their bicycles about with them on every holiday. They could ride for miles without supervision in the royal gardens at Frogmore in another part of Windsor Great Park, and a small parcel of food usually accompanied them on these outings. Neither child thought anything of a spill and cut knee, and they liked to show off at riding without touching the handlebars.

Princess Elizabeth had become quite a good cook, her bent being to things she could do with her hands. She took cooking lessons in the Royal Lodge kitchens and practised in her Welsh cottage.

She sent cakes she had made and iced to children in hospitals or in unemployed areas. She could also sweep, dust, and scrub properly. She kept her play-cottage clean, and when giving a tea-party there, polished the furniture, calling in Queen Mary, a frequent visitor and keen housewife, to admire the result.

One of the great advantages of Royal Lodge from the Princesses' point of view was that their mother was not always doing important things that kept her from them. Her good-tempered patience never failed in spite of their continual interruptions on what was also her holiday. She prized her week-end leisure with them and the opportunities it gave for influencing and directing their outlook on life.

IX

Queen Mary as Guide

THE three glittering pre-war years, 1937, 1938, and 1939, spent by the Princesses at Buckingham Palace, took them out of the simple environment on which their parents had always insisted and provided them with a background of royalty that for the time being became inevitable because they were the King's daughters.

With the capacity of children for taking things for granted they soon grew used to the glamour, once it became an everyday affair. They found Queen Mary's educational Monday afternoon tours far more interesting than the most brilliant Court happenings.

There was nothing royal about these visits to museums, galleries, and other national institutions. Queen Mary had planned them for months and started them as soon as the children returned from their summer holidays. She took them unannounced among other sightseers, and people got used to finding the small party looking at the same pictures or statues as they. First they " did " the Tower, where they saw their father's crowns back in place in the Jewel House.

A month later Queen Mary walked them up the British Museum steps and they learnt a bit about Assyria and the times of the Pharaohs.

So much for history. Their grandmother wanted them to know contemporary life as well, and took them over the Mint to see how money was made.

Going ahead of events for the moment, Queen Mary continued this programme up to the war, usually accompanying her grandchildren herself or, if not, sending a lady-in-waiting. Princess Elizabeth did the post office without her sister, entered the control cabin of the driverless electric train that takes letters from London's giant sorting office at Mount Pleasant to railway termini. The Princesses saw the Science Museum working models and the picture galleries. Princess Elizabeth's interest in pictures and art exhibitions (she has been to the Royal Academy) is genuine because she paints herself. I am told by a friend of the Queen's that her little flower paintings and landscapes are really talented.

It was not until shortly before the war that Queen Mary fell in with the Princesses' wish to ride on an underground train. Their parents were then away in Canada, the family had never had a real separation since Princess Elizabeth was a baby, and something had to be done to cheer the children up. They were taken in an Inner Circle train, sat in a third-class smoking carriage, got out and on to an escalator for the first time in their lives—Princess Margaret getting on wrongly with her right foot—then into a tube train. Margaret got the tickets

PRINCESS MARGARET ROSE ENJOYS A BOOK AT WINDSOR CASTLE.
Jane is not usually allowed to lie on the couch, but was permitted this short spell of bliss for
the sake of the picture.

from a machine, paying half fare for herself and her sister, and there was an exciting moment when the inspector, not knowing who they were, ran after them for failing to give them up.

Can you guess the one place in London about which the Princesses knew more than Queen Mary ? It was, of course, the Zoo. They knew the animals, old and new, had held most of the Zoo babies, and were familiar with the habits of creatures from cobras to chimpanzees.

All the keepers were used to seeing the children walking among the crowds with their nurse and perhaps a party of small friends, especially on Monday when the entrance money was sixpence instead of a shilling. Hatless and on warm days coatless, the Princesses would run from house to house, explaining their animal friends to their other friends, refusing guides because they knew exactly where to go, but greeting all the keepers, who took them inside the houses. Keepers considered Princess Elizabeth almost their equal in handling animals ; she was quite fearless. She knew a lot about the habits of snakes, and the keeper would stir up a cobra so that the children could see it striking.

On one three-hour visit the Princesses saw the garments sent by admirers of a chimpanzee, Booboo, for her baby, and a toothbrush for Jubilee's first tooth. They nursed a baby alligator and tickled the puffer fish to see them inflate themselves. They knew the Pets' Corner well and Princess Elizabeth was allowed to feed a baby bear on condensed milk. Once she was lecturing her sister for giving Rani and another elephant, Sally, too many buns at once when, with peals of laughter from Margaret, Rani reached out her trunk and took the whole bag of buns from the lecturer.

The King and Queen hold no brief for the tears caused in the royal schoolroom nearly a century ago by Queen Victoria, who insisted on educating her children regardless of temperament " to resemble in every respect their dearest beloved Papa." A well-balanced day in which minds and bodies have equal chance for development is the basis on which the Princesses' general upbringing is planned. The King and Cabinet divide the emphasis between priming Princess Elizabeth in Empire and constitutional history and seeing that she has a command of languages and on her growing up with a modern sports-loving outlook and understanding of widely differing points of view.

Lessons begin now for both Princesses in their separate classrooms at 9.30 and finish at 12.45, with 15 minutes for break in the middle of the morning. Exercise and special classes take up the afternoons.

Princess Elizabeth combines intelligence with a capacity for hard work. She has a practical outlook. She has succeeded in acquiring a good mastery, for her age, of French—thanks to an able tutor, and to a " French only " day once a week.

Geography, with history interwoven to link places and events in the modern manner, and essay-writing, sums and also English grammar, dictation and Scripture are taken by Miss Crawford.

94

All languages are taught by tutors, and both the Princesses have special tuition in music.

The Princess was old enough during those years at the Palace to benefit from talks with statesmen on current affairs. Her coaching in constitutional law and history now that she is older includes study of the King's powers and functions, which she will have to exercise some day. She has been taught how a Royal Proclamation is made. How her father would dissolve Parliament. When he uses the Great Seal, as in the case of a treaty. How Cabinet Ministers enter his service by kissing his hands and hand back their seals of office on relinquishing their posts.

Princess Margaret has the same French tutor as her sister and speaks quite fluently. She is, perhaps, the more musical of the two; possesses, like her elder sister, a good memory, and her genius for mimicry keeps relatives amused.

After the move to the Palace, dancing classes were held there as before on Tuesdays. On Wednesday afternoons the Princesses changed into Girl Guide and Brownie uniforms under the expert eye of a headquarters official, Miss Synge, the King insisting on the importance of any uniform being worn correctly.

The Queen had been a District Commissioner in the Girl Guides, and their aunt, the Princess Royal, was the Association's president, and when Princess Elizabeth wanted to make knots and track as some of her friends were doing, the Buckingham Palace Company was formed. A spick and span hand-cart painted navy blue with the company's name in gold lettering arrived, and the Princess Royal enrolled her elder niece in the Kingfisher Patrol and the younger as a Brownie in the Leprechaun Six.

Guides and Brownies at Wednesday's gatherings were recruited from the Princesses' friends and relatives, including Queen Mary's great-niece, Lady Mary Cambridge, and from the daughters of employees at the Palace. As the old summer-house of George the Fifth was in decay and the second-floor Palace schoolroom did not seem a good substitute, the King promised his daughters a new play-house in the Palace grounds. He kept his word. The new summer-house was started a year later, but before the Princesses could use the charming little place with one large room and big windows, war had broken out.

The Palace Guides, including Elizabeth, had soon earned their nature, housewifery, and cookery badges, learnt to tie knots and signal in Morse, and planned to track and study woodcraft at Windsor. They paid twopence a week subscription, with which signalling flags and stationery were bought.

That winter of 1937 the Buckingham Palace Company did a Christmas-stocking trail for families in distressed areas and collected toys, clothes, and sweets.

THE PRINCESSES AND THE GIRL GUIDES.

The Princesses continue the association of the Royal Family with the Girl Guide movement. The top photograph shows the King and Queen with Queen Mary, Princess Elizabeth and Princess Margaret Rose at a Royal review of Girl Guides at Windsor.

Right: Final adjustments to Princess Elizabeth's uniform, while her sister, in Brownie uniform, looks on.

[*Photos : Topical and Graphic Photo Union*

G

state visits at Buckingham Palace. Princess Elizabeth now

X

Training in Hostess-ship

BY 1938 the Empire had settled down to the change
of rulers, but with the sands running out in
Europe and heads of states in constant conference
over Hitler's threat to invade Czecho-Slovakia,
London was in the thick of diplomatic moves. In
one month four of Europe's kings, a regent, and crown prince
were at Buckingham Palace.

As in the days before the King's accession, the royal
family snatched what time they could together, sharing the
interest and pleasure of " wonderful and lovely things," as
Princess Elizabeth would say. A visit, for instance, to the queer,
white, ship-shaped building in Portland Place, Broadcasting
House, to see how the Children's Hour was done, and a tour
of the first big exhibition the Princesses had seen, at Glasgow,
where they signed a visitors' book. That same day at Glasgow,
while all the world watched Germany, the Princesses went
with their mother when she launched the giant Cunarder, *Queen
Elizabeth*, at Clydebank, and marvelled as the great form moved
between crowded shores. Two days later, at Munich, Chamberlain, Hitler, Mussolini, and Daladier signed a peaceful agreement

by which it was hoped to give Hitler what he wanted without bringing about a European war.

The Queen was busier than her daughters liked her to be. Two or three mornings a week had to be allotted to her dress-makers in preparation for a State visit to Paris and other State visits at Buckingham Palace. Princess Elizabeth, now promoted from lunch in the nursery to taking the meal with her parents, was often beside herself with hunger when 1.15 came and, looking in at her mother's drawing-room, she saw her still surrounded by fitter, dress designer, pins, and half-made clothes, and the prospects of lunch apparently remote.

That spring brought Princess Elizabeth's promotion to silk stockings and her mother gave her a boxful for her twelfth birthday. She wore them to match her champagne-coloured shoes at the wedding of her cousin, Anne Bowes-Lyon, to Viscount Anson. Their grandmother, Lady Strathmore, whose one thought was that Anne's wedding-dress should be as lovely as Elizabeth's (the Queen's), was too ill to see her wear it at the ceremony, and her death that summer caused the post-ponement till July of the State visit to Paris.

The passing of the warm-hearted, lovable woman whose charm is inherited by the Queen, was a deep sorrow to older and younger members of the royal family. Her memory will ever be linked with happy childhood, not only that of the Queen but the Princesses, for they spent joyous holidays with her on many occasions.

By now the Princesses had got used to the big Palace parties at which attendance was a privilege, and they were a real help to their mother at the huge Royal Garden Party for twelve thousand. The Queen was very sad and was to have kept away, but at the last minute the King developed gastric influenza, and she had to take his place and greet the guests with her usual smile.

Crowds who saw off the King and Queen when they left for Paris included the girls who for weeks had worked overtime on the beautiful white crinolines, copied from the Palace corridor portraits and destined to captivate the Parisians. Two years later the swastika was to fly over the historic Palace of Versailles, where much of the entertaining for the royal guests took place.

When embroideresses and sempstresses reached their London workrooms they found a large box of red roses as a " thank you " from the Queen.

Red roses, which were not favoured at No. 145 Piccadilly, were used a great deal in entertaining at the Palace as the symbolic flower of England. They provided Princess Elizabeth with a quaint reason for being glad that she was no longer a Princess " of York." Anxious to be loyal to her " side," she had always refused them if offered her, with the firm reply, " I'm York," which made people laugh.

After a summer without pause, the King took his family for a holiday where neither letters, cables, nor State documents could find him, on the royal yacht *Victoria and Albert*. The Princesses loved the sailors—there was a crew of three hundred.

They swam and sunbathed. They enjoyed taking part in conferences on the ship's course, decided each day by their father, mother, and the ship's commander, Sir Dudley North, who in another year would be directing the Navy at war.

The new glass-roofed sports annexe at Buckingham Palace, built on the site of an old racquets court, was complete with swimming pool and chlorination plant for the Princesses' daily swim on their return from Balmoral that summer. Glamis that year without their grandmother to plan surprises had seemed lonely and dreary.

Buckingham Palace had been made particularly spick and span for all the kings who were coming. King Carol was to stay there with Prince Michael. King George of Greece and King Haakon of Norway would be paying calls from their hotels. Prince Paul, Regent of Jugo-Slavia, and the Crown Prince of Sweden were also coming to London.

The famous guest rooms, the Belgian Suite, had had a special " spring " clean—this always takes place in August at the Palace—and was looking its rather old-fashioned but splendid best. Princess Elizabeth and Princess Margaret made no secret of their views that most of the Palace was too " red plush," and when, on one occasion, they heard a Lancashire boy allude, in a recitation in the broad speech of his county, to the Palace being " all marble busts and plush," they burst into approving laughter.

Whenever the Palace was seething with doings and Princess Elizabeth and Princess Margaret could get no attention, they

THE ROYAL FAMILY ON BOARD THE " VICTORIA AND ALBERT " DURING A
CRUISING HOLIDAY.

ran to some large wooden boxes that stood opened but unpacked and were addressed to them. They contained the Paris miniature model gowns, coats, and hats, the real jewels and furs of " France " and " Marianne," the two beautiful, three-foot high dolls, with tightly curled hair and sweeping eyelashes, sent to them by the children of France in memory of their parents' visit to Paris. It was an inexhaustible thrill to dip one's hand in among the wrappings and see what came out next ; it might be anything from an oiled silk umbrella to a tiny white Ascot gown with gold embroidery.

Later that year the Princesses, with the help of Court officials, organised an exhibition for the first time, and the dolls and their belongings were on view and seen at St. James's Palace by 23,000 people.

Neither of the Princesses " approved " of their father's birthday being celebrated in June, six months before it happened, and ignored on December 14th. They arranged with their parents that their children's Christmas party should always be on that day so that it could be in his honour as well. It was at any rate a good plan for ensuring his presence at the party, for he was a great success with children. This function became real training for hostess-ship for the royal children. The Queen let them plan it as far as possible themselves. They held conferences in Princess Elizabeth's den. Careful attention was paid to the buffet. They asked for hot chocolate and iced fresh fruit orange and lemon drinks for the children, and tea for parents and nannies. They had equally definite views on food.

There MUST be chocolate éclairs and meringues in addition to little iced cakes in all sorts of crescent and heart shapes.

The Princesses received their small guests standing beside their parents. The child visitors curtsied or bowed first to the King, then to the Queen, and then to the Princesses. When the Princesses were small, their father hired a miniature merry-go-round and chute for their parties. As they grew older a show was always given, sometimes a film, at other times a marionette show or Punch and Judy. Hide-and-seek usually wound up proceedings.

With all this entertaining for State visitors and nursery folk, the Princesses learnt to be always at ease and friendly with every one. Mr. Joseph Kennedy, the American Ambassador in London, thought them the best behaved children he had met.

Six months before war broke out, March 1939, Buckingham Palace was again as busy as an hotel at the height of the season, with the Queen having to turn out some of her own attendants for bedrooms for the staff of her guests, the President of the French Republic and Mme Lebrun. For its size, Buckingham Palace has not a great number of guest rooms. This was a visit of special importance, and as the French farmer's son fastened in his coat each evening the buttonhole sent up for him from the royal gardens in Windsor Great Park, he little dreamed that in another fifteen months the soil of his beloved France would be handed over to the German invader.

Princess Elizabeth was now thirteen and there was a subtle

change in the way she was treated. She would soon be as tall as her mother. The Queen no longer dressed her in the babyish bonnet-shaped hats still worn by Princess Margaret ; she had smartly tilted caps very like those being worn by her elders and her coats and frocks were made to below her knees.

On her birthday, at Windsor as usual, a special messenger arrived at the Castle with her ever-growing mail, and the Director of Music of the Guards Band sent an orderly to ask her what music she would like. She chose *Rose Marie*.

She had presented prizes several times, rosettes to child winners at pony shows and cups and shields in children's swimming competitions at the Bath Club. She was allowed to take up her first activity, presidency of the Children's League of the Princess Elizabeth of York Hospital.

The Princess's sympathy was readily fostered for other children. To be sorry for children who were sick and in hospital or whose parents were unemployed and who had few sweets and toys was synonymous with wanting to do something practical to help. This eager desire was always directed with great care and encouraged in ways most suited to her years.

In addition to her own hospital there were many others in which a children's ward had been named after her, and in this way she began to learn something about hospital organisation up and down the country.

She had not yet stayed up to dinner, but the night before her parents left for Canada, did the nearest thing to it—helped

them receive their dinner guests. When the grown-ups had
gone in to dine, Princess Elizabeth went upstairs, took off
her party frock, had her bath and then her simple supper
before going to bed. The bedtime routine for the royal children
is bath before food.

THE KING RIDING WITH HIS DAUGHTERS.

A photograph taken at Windsor on Princess Elizabeth's thirteenth birthday.

XI

King and Queen Calling

THE life of this royal family was about to be broken up. Monarchy exacts harsh sacrifices. King and Queen and their daughters had gone unitedly through the breathless changes of the last three years. In accepting the Crown, the King assumed heavy, inescapable duties.

The visit of the King and Queen to Canada and the United States in May and June 1939 was the beginning of long periods of separation. Although Canada's allegiance to the Empire is vested solely in the Crown, no British sovereign had ever spent so much as a day in that vast country. The royal programme would be exhausting; it was impossible for the King and Queen to take their daughters but they promised that they would one day return with them.

" If they go," people at the Palace were saying, prepared for war to break out between England, France, and Germany five months before it actually did. The King and Queen were determined, if possible, to keep their promise to visit Canada, which had been preparing a magnificent welcome for months.

On the day of departure, May 6th, on the liner *Empress*

of Australia, after driving through Portsmouth's crowded, cheering streets, the King and Queen showed the Princesses over their cabins. Three o'clock struck, the hour at which the liner was supposed to sail, and the children and the rest of the royal family were still on board. The King had to tell them it was time to leave. The Princesses returned to the jetty, Margaret's face puckered up, Elizabeth looked tearful, the crowds roared their cheers, guns thundered, ships' sirens shrieked, engines of twenty-seven bombers droned overhead, and, a brave sight with its escort of warships, the royal ship made for the open sea, King and Queen gazing until the two little figures merged into the blur of thronged quays.

As Queen Mary had not been in the best of health she could not undertake the charge of her granddaughters, although she intended to take them about with her to save them from missing their parents unduly. Schoolroom life continued much as usual for the Princesses. A detective was appointed as a special bodyguard for the seven weeks of the King's and Queen's absence. The Princesses spent most of the time at Buckingham Palace, with week-ends at St. Paul's, Walden-bury, Hertfordshire house where the Queen was born, now occupied by her brother David, whom as a child she used to " mother."

Letters and cables were exchanged almost daily between the royal travellers and their children. After tea the Princesses wrote to their parents and kept diaries to show the King and Queen on their return. Princess Elizabeth sent her mother snaps and made a film of her sister and their pets with the aid of a ciné camera. Children like their parents to be a success. The King and Queen won the hearts of the North American peoples, and their triumphant procession was followed with satisfaction by the two little girls in England.

They read all the Press eulogies and were thrilled by photographs of their mother looking both beautiful and majestic in gracious crinolines which they had last seen hung all over Palace rooms awaiting packing in special cases large enough for the hoops to lie flat on top of each other.

Naturally certain incidents in the tour appealed to their youthful imaginations more than others. They wanted to hear all about the Red Indian encampment visited by their parents, about the Dionne quin who gave her bouquet to their father instead of to their mother. Elizabeth's history was sufficiently advanced to follow with interest her parents' visit to George Washington's tomb.

The Princesses, three thousand miles away, had a quarter of an hour's share in the dovetailed programme of their parents' visit to Ottawa, Canada's capital. The King and Queen were to call them up on Sunday afternoon.

All arrangements were complete for the link-up between the New World city of beautiful buildings and the large house in Hertfordshire's park-like countryside, St. Paul's, Waldenbury, from which the Princesses were to speak. The day was a most exciting one for the two children. Princess Elizabeth was at home with long-distance calls to Scotland or occasionally the Continent, but Princess Margaret was still too young to manage even a local call without a struggle.

The royal priority call would come through at three o'clock. They would share an instrument but two hand microphones had been installed in the drawing-room of Government House at Ottawa so that the King and Queen could each hear everything that the children said.

" Whitwell 25 is on the line. The Princesses are waiting."

The moment had come, and both the little girls had the delight of hearing their parents' voices, and though Princess Margaret was shy in her replies, her elder sister managed to bridge the Atlantic to her satisfaction.

Princess Elizabeth held the receiver first. Her mother was speaking, asking how she and Margaret were, telling her that it was ten in the morning and that daddy and she were just going off on official duties. Then her father's voice came through.

Princess Margaret managed to give Queen Mary's love, to say that she was having a nice time but would be glad when they came home, and then it was time for their uncle, the Hon. David Bowes-Lyon, to speak and lastly Elizabeth again. The magic quarter of an hour in which a large part of the earth had been girdled, was over.

The King and Queen had spent many and interesting weeks in the new world where monarchy, like other institutions, had to prove present-day usefulness. Their personal success undoubtedly raised the valuation overseas of the Crown as an

[Photo: Fox Photos Ltd.

THE KING AND QUEEN AND THE TWO PRINCESSES JOIN IN THE SINGING
AT THE KING'S CAMP ON ABERGELDIE ESTATE, BALMORAL.

asset in the leadership of peoples. A splendid welcome home was staged as the British nation's tribute to achievement. The Cabinet decided that the Princesses must have a prominent share in the official reception. It was arranged that the two children should be taken out by destroyer to greet their parents at sea.

It was a wonderful trip. Blue eyes sparkling, hair blowing, the little girls were piped on board the *Kempenfelt*, shook hands with the officers, and journeyed out to meet the *Empress of Britain*, the liner chosen for the return trip, as it awaited them in the Solent.

A naval barge took them off the destroyer and they were soon running up the companion-way of the royal ship, shouting, " Hullo, Mummy ! Hullo, Daddy ! we had a lovely time on the destroyer." It was a truly joyous re-union.

Princess Elizabeth was beginning to know both the Fleet and the Merchant Navy. It was necessary that a future ruler of the British Empire should do so. At Spithead she had seen the whole fleet in the historic roadstead, with ships of other nations, at the Coronation review. She could point out the distinguishing features of battleships, destroyers, and aircraft carriers. She had toured London and Southampton docks and seen something of the system of seaborne trade, she had been shown the last word in floating hotels, the *Queen Mary* and *Queen Elizabeth*. And she was getting to know the sea from the point of view of pleasure yachting. This year she was to see Dartmouth, to which King, Queen, and their daughters sailed in the royal yacht for the King to inspect the Royal Naval College cadets.

Britain holidayed as usual that August on the eve of war. There was an intensified pleasure about that holiday, remarked on by many people at the time, an odd sensation of happiness snatched from the agonising months that, it was rightly feared, were to come. At Balmoral as elsewhere, those were happy days, with an amazingly simple plan of life in which the royal family and their guests came and went with the mood of the moment, ate when they liked, meals being shorn of formality.

Often the sole excitement in the Princesses' day was driving their pony cart themselves to the village and back. They love this method of travel and have kept it up since coming south. Walkers in the park near their wartime home meet the two little girls jogging along, hatless, laughing, and talking merrily, taking it in turns to hold the reins, which they do gracefully with ribbons threaded in orthodox fashion over the first finger and under the thumb of the left hand.

The two royal children took the keenest interest in the King's Camp and attended the boys' concerts. The King had two hundred schoolboys from public and council schools staying on the Balmoral estate. He taught them map-reading and led them on seventeen-mile walks.

The Princesses were beginning to talk about the new term at Buckingham Palace and the departure of their cousins Prince Edward and Princess Alexandra for Australia. The royal babies would leave England by liner before their parents, who were to fly part of the way. They would spend Christmas in Australia instead of at Sandringham, the Duke of Kent having been appointed Governor-General.

The little Prince and his sister, however, never left home. Wooden cases of nursery toys had to be unpacked. His small brown pony, Farino, a few months older than he, continued to graze at Coppins instead of being sent off in a wooden crate.

The two little girls at Balmoral did not come south that autumn. England and France declared war in September, and Britain's first thought was to safeguard its childhood in the months of aerial attack which were believed imminent.

XII

Evacuees

ROYAL children cannot escape from the path of the avalanche called History, and when war came, it changed overnight the Princesses' homes, habits, friends, interests, and all the plans being made for them.

The King and Queen at Buckingham Palace sorrowfully watched Great Britain enter war on a September Sunday morning of 1939. Their children were still at Balmoral and they knew that it might be months before they saw them again.

It was a hard decision to leave them there, especially for the Queen, but the sacrifice was made primarily to convince other parents of the necessity of sending their children to safe areas. If the King and Queen had consulted their inclination and brought the Princesses back to London, other parents would have kept their children in danger zones, with less protection possibly against air attack than the Palace possessed in its network of cellars. Princess Elizabeth and Princess Margaret were evacuees from the first day of war.

Later the King and Queen made better arrangements.

120

PRINCESS ELIZABETH AND PRINCESS MARGARET ROSE IN THEIR WAR-TIME HOME.

Balmoral was too far and though the two children were very happy in the Highlands the King could not spare time to go there. The Queen saw her daughters once between September and Christmas, which was spent as usual at Sandringham. They were sent in the New Year of 1940 to Royal Lodge, Windsor being a reception area. The Royal Family were able to spend future week-ends together.

A shelter under the lawn at Royal Lodge had been turfed over and equipped with wireless. The Princesses planned air raid procedure for their pets, and were delighted to hear that their father had done what he could for London animals by making the Palace mews a hospital for horses, ponies, and donkeys injured in raids in Westminster.

The Princesses' national service included being useful in the home. Neither child expected to be waited on. The Queen had brought up her daughters to remember and do things for themselves and not to give unnecessary trouble. This training had special advantages in war-time when staffs in royal as in other homes were depleted as a result of the calling up of young men. The Princesses made their own beds. They wrapped up and addressed their own parcels.

The two little girls were glad to be at bright and modern Royal Lodge, their favourite home, and near their parents. As the Queen said, they had " missed their Mummy and Daddy very much " at Balmoral. They had their ponies and dogs at Windsor and occasionally made a day trip to London for some family celebration at the Palace.

These peace-time activities, however, soon took second place and they became enthusiastic little war-workers. Their mother had Wednesday afternoon sewing-bees at the Palace, Queen Mary was entertaining soldiers in the west country, the Princess Royal went about in uniform inspecting women in the services, the Duchess of Gloucester toured Red Cross depots, and the Duchess of Kent rolled bandages.

The Princesses caught the fever. They knitted daily, went in for war savings, and, since they could no longer gather sphagnum moss which they had got in Scotland for surgical dressings, collected waste-paper and rags.

Both are neat knitters. Princess Elizabeth had for years made baby coats and scarves, and Princess Margaret scarves, for their grandmother's charities. They now knitted comforts first for Finnish children and then for the British Expeditionary Force.

They put by as much pocket money as possible each week. They bought with it war savings and tobacco for soldiers. The two little girls, like both their parents, are full of lovable impulses to help others.

They took to heart the cause of child evacuees, sending their own coats and frocks to British children in reception areas. They asked East End girls evacuated to Windsor to tea at Royal Lodge ; they knew them through the 10th Windsor Girl Guide Troop, to which they now belonged as the Buckingham Palace Troop was disbanded. They also took part in children's concerts for war charities.

Willingness to help in local good causes was one direct effect of the personal training given to their children by the King and Queen. The royal parents lay stress on the importance of that branch of social service that comes under the heading of neighbourliness. While still at their home in Scotland they had helped in parish work under the direction of the Rev. and Mrs. John Lamb, minister at Crathie Church, which the King and his family attend when at Balmoral. Mr. Lamb is His Majesty's Domestic Chaplain in Scotland.

The Princesses' activities there were largely on behalf of evacuated children, and gifts of clothing in particular had been needed. When the Princesses came down south, they again were allowed and encouraged to help work for war charities.

Village hall concerts were organised in which the Princesses and other children took part, the mothers making up an enthusiastic part of the audience. All the child performers thoroughly enjoyed themselves, and in between the items the Queen talked to the other mothers, congratulating them on their children's performances.

The Princesses came in for their share of praise. Both took part in sketches and in a ballet with other children. They gave a tap dance together. Princess Elizabeth performed a dance solo and Princess Margaret a pianoforte solo. One of the sketches in which they acted was from *Alice in Wonderland*, and Princess Margaret took the role of Dormouse.

The younger Princess's first wartime birthday was celebrated in the south instead of in Scotland. It is in August, and as iced cakes had by then been officially banned, her birthday cake was a chocolate sponge affair, chocolate covering being permitted. The King and Queen, the Princesses, and some of their friends picnicked in honour of the day in a secluded spot in a forest a few miles away from the royal family home.

Another of the Princesses' war activities was saving metal. They responded to the appeal for aluminium for aircraft by giving utensils belonging to them both from Princess Elizabeth's miniature cottage at Royal Lodge.

The Princesses, like most childrem, love a day on the river. On fine summer afternoons they sometimes cruise on a motor launch along the upper reaches of the Thames. Once they accompanied the King and Queen on an inspection of the river's Home Guard, the Upper Thames Patrol. At each lock a guard of honour of small boats was formed.

The royal children took a keen and intelligent interest in the progress of the war, for which a few minutes' discussion was allotted regularly in the school time-table. They read with interest the newspaper accounts of their father's visit to France. They listened-in to their mother's broadcasts, and, among others, worried over the feared fate of the three hundred thousand soldiers rescued from Dunkirk beaches by the oddest of English armadas and sent sweets as a practical expression of their admiration.

The Princesses delighted to make new friends. In the

democratic life at Windsor, they mixed with children who gave them new points of view. They were drawn from homes in the neighbourhood and for the most part knew nothing of Court life. It was another of those beneficial experiences that so often came their way and brought them the pleasures of companionship that all children need for a normal healthy life.

In happier times the nation will renew the acquaintance of " the little Princesses" whose small figures flitted charmingly for years in and out of the pages of pre-war history. One felt that it would always be so, that these engaging little people would never grow up. They are doing so rapidly, however, while the public's back is turned.

Let us leave them on the porch at Royal Lodge on a spring morning, looking down the wide drive where large whitewashed stones have been placed, as on a coastguard station path, to guide cars and footsteps in the black-out. Around them the almond trees planted by the Queen are a mass of exquisite pink blossom. One suddenly sees how free the life of these modern royal children has been, although so carefully directed. One realises, too, that should they fulfil their promise, the nation will owe a great debt to the man and woman who have trained them so perfectly for their future—the King and Queen.

Princess Elizabeth, tall and self-possessed, is looking more like Queen Mary than ever, and one reads in the winningly serious little face that genius for duty that made a great king of the very ordinary man who was George the Fifth. There is merriment in her eyes, and friendliness and kindliness too. At her feet sit the inevitable Corgis. And beside her Princess Margaret, a small, dainty figure, bubbles over with laughter, reminding you that to Princesses, as to other children, life is sweet.

THE END

Printed by Morrison & Gibb, Ltd., London & Edinburgh